The Book of Stolen Images

The Book of Stolen Images

Laura Lee Washburn

Meadowlark
PRESS
Emporia, Kansas, USA

Meadowlark Press, LLC
meadowlarkpoetrypress.com
P.O. Box 333, Emporia, KS 66801

The Book of Stolen Images
Copyright © Laura Lee Washburn, 2023

Cover art by Tino Rodriguez, "The Luminous Radiance of a Spring Lullaby," watercolor and gouache on paper, 24" x 36", 2011
www.tinorodriguez.com, Instagram: tinorodriguezartist

Cover design by TMS, Meadowlark Press

Author photo by Sam Clausen

Interior design by Linzi Garcia, Meadowlark Press

POETRY / Women Authors
POETRY / American / General
POETRY / Subjects & Themes / General

ISBN: 978-1-956578-35-5
Library of Congress Control Number: 2023933318

for the ones we've lost and the ones that go on living

Table of Contents

III: The First Dog

IV: Snouts and Bristles

The Immortal Dragon

Philosophy

I am an inverted tree, my roots reaching into the air.
What stops me from looking for God
may be the same gravity that perches me on Earth.
I look a long while at the blaze of green

before I go down to disintegrate. Bark
and branches grow me, inside and out.
Like the Hanged Man of the Tarot, I arc
in perfect symbol, content as the reckless beetle.

Make no mistake; don't think his one foot snared
is a confusion of punishment and stasis.
He, like I, was meant to wake, to find simple fears,

to crawl out of the burrow and grope
with only crossed arms for a shield.

Self-Portrait in First Grade

Lucky child, we have been dreams together
with eyes bright as birthstone sapphires.
When we clasped hands in the white
muff, the rabbit's fur sold us on its pleasure.

I was like nothing then I would ever be again.
The caterpillar I portrayed in kindergarten
in dyed green Keds was going to transform
into a bookish woman, at least that segment
connected to my feet. I know some
legs and arms went military or complacent,
took drugs, cancer-died, built machines.

We were the child the neighbors came
to take pictures of at the bus stop, blond-eyed
and blue or however that goes, perfected
in purple gingham like any mother's favorite doll.
Did I mention patent leather?

This isn't a brag, the hair and eyes,
the dress, the absolute black shoes
are symbols. Was I even there to wear them?

Imagine being welcomed like that child,
imagine her fear of entering the yellow bus alone,
imagine the flash of the portrait,
the not-yellow of her teeth, the blue bus number
pinned to the frilled pinafore.

I would like human frailty to amuse me;
I would like to stop her constant
disappointment. I am like the dog
who can't stop biting at the flea, the one
whose skin welts up, the one who bleeds
from the actions of his own nails and teeth.

The child is going into the halls where one boy
always gets in trouble, where the teachers
rip off his cap to find his father
shaved him bald, where skin colors
don't match and all hair doesn't hang straight,
where she finds meanesses are cultivated,
where she learns to read the first word,
where in small chairs they strain to say it:
I, I, I.

Toadstools

"toadstools slide, each on the other" —Marianne Moore

Last night in the yard I spotted a toad.
He explained the cracking twig at the backdoor

in the dark and suburban quiet.
The dog is almost blind. The toad slipped

away in fright. Walking off my anger Saturday
before, we found the unexpected September damp

had left white mushrooms, phalluses and patio
umbrellas in miniature, one sliding under the other,

and this gave us new purpose for our stride, sighting
each one and then more, the striped brown, the large, puffball,

chanterelle, and one a loaf grown from the slimmest
sidewalk crack, and there a dozen kicked by child or man.

I never saw a toad amongst the stools. The dog
remained oblivious. My anger, never gone,
I'm simply tired of talking, not sure that story's worth the tell.

Instead think fairies, organisms, fungi, mold,
lawyer's wig, Judas' ear, the smooth chanterelle,

trumpet of death, snowbank false, inky cap,
tough velvet foot, hens of the woods: all these mushrooms
    living spells.

Peace and Reckoning

i. Of Whom to Beware

Every English teacher has a brother with a gun,
somebody who goes out Thanksgiving for a duck.

The teachers sit home with red pens, or so you would suppose.
They're planning the future, looking for odd Oxford commas.

ii. National Accountability & Death

Listen up: all the English teachers have taken notice.
If the indicators of fire suggest accelerant,
everything so quick, who wouldn't believe
he killed his wife and kids?
                                        But the burn marks
never indicated arson, so we're killing
the wrong man again. The fire science
failure to understand plastics. Don't worry,
he's black or, anyway, poor.

All the death row murderers lie down in orange jumpsuits
and sleep until their last meal, the fried legs
of chicken, processed meat in a shell,
beans and gravy, fatback, boiled tongue, ribs.

iii. Nonviolent Means, the Chemical Plans: Exigency

All the lies about the country are coming true.
All the truths about the country are becoming lies.
They'll pull Granny up by her bootstraps before they knock
    her down.

You can see every lie from your seat in the house.
Like the good Dr. King, link your arms with your neighbors.
Every English teacher has *that* violence inside.

See these violent sit on the ground. They point their eyes
like accusations. Have even you never wanted
to drop the stiffening toddler into bed as he resists?

When the officers come, they'll aim red cans.
Last summer you covered your mouth and sprayed at the fleas
    in the carpet.

They'll tilt back your head and spray
your bloody throat. Haven't you, Poet, been heard to sing
    overcome?

The yellow spray is trained on your classroom
of literature bullies. You were taught to leave
when the poet smelled burning almonds.

    Oh, Little Miss Lee, why don't you ever have a gun?
    Your baby doll is marked and torn. The red stitches
    have broken where he sewed on the arm.

Traitors to the state train for empathy.
Sonny's glass trembles over the piano. The old
woman blows out the light. The fawn, still
warm in the belly, cracks at each jut
of the rock. The cat in the basket is going to leap.

Another three barns are burning. You've wanted the park
and the pantomime, the stage dog, and the wink
in the eye of the rogue.

Landmines and unmanned drones, baton carriers,
riot gear masks, zip cuffs, the boot in the neck or the face:
let the distractions be football or poems, the witty turn
of phrase. They're coming with cages and bans.
They're coming, zip ties and false flags, they're coming,
    they're here.

Blackbirds

Sometimes dark birds fly into the walls of our house,
and we hear them scuttling between plaster and brick,
reduced to crawling or climbing after their magic trick.

Out the window, we catch their shadows lining up.
The cats' eyes glint as they rush from supper
to their work: first bird song, then the cats' alert song.

No one will ever see a grackle slide between the bricks,
that slight of wing is from another physics.
Yet walking up the stairs, we hear their talons next to us,

hear the frantic and desperate scramble when we speak.
Something wants out of this house and this time.
Something that wanted a nest now wants air.

The Gathering

*"There will be another eye, a strange one, beside
our own: unspeaking under its stony lid." —Paul Celan*

When the old man comes dragging his sack,
the children run away from the fire.
Sparks snap and glide, then fade. Whole worlds
whistle and break. Even under the perigee moon,
the woods are dark. Moonlight berries soothe
and lure.   *Children run away from the fire!*
The old man has come dragging his sack.

When he drops back into his crevice
and rock, he drags the deep sack behind him.
The gray stone of the third eye knows
in its slow blink every terror in our skulls.
   Hands reach up
to cup us as we gather. Hands reach up,
but dumb, we run away from the fires.

Parable

Once a miller lived with a tailor
in great contentment. They washed
clothes together and spun thread
while bread baked. One day

an ogre knocked a rock
against their pale oak door.
A dog leapt at the back window.
A nixie peered out of their stream.

The king's son came with shoes
that needed mending. A beautiful
woman disguised herself
as a witch. The wolf was heard

to howl in the nearby forest.
They lost everything they had,
the grain soured, the needles broke,
the internet shut down, their health

insurance was cut off. No one
noticed them with cardboard signs
on the street. The weather turned.
The Muslims left the cities.

A wall went up. Women grew fat
with pregnancy. A giant farted.
Fireworks simmered a hole
in the shut-down pharmacy.

No simple ending comes. No
one buys your extra plates.
The canned food will run out;
maybe the food bank offers more.

Mother Duck

Oh, oh, my life, my loves.
Oh, oh, my life, my loves.

A woman turned into a duck
might care for the three eggs
on the bank, might swim circles in pond,
eat fish. A witch turned
into a good woman might slice the necks
of three young ducks.

What is there but crying when
       through no fault of anyone

       Oh, oh, my life my love,
       all things beautiful in my life

the good man goes. Maybe he leaves her
entombed in his good house. Maybe he
tells her always to wait. Maybe
he sends her to Spain, maybe he intends.

When the three ducklings lie throats
slit to bellies on the floor,
when the three good young children
are dead, she might finally come back
calling, Oh, oh, my life, my loves.
Oh, oh, my life   finally true,
finally not settled in anyone's trap
but calling the pure grief of soul.

A witch often comes to no.
A good woman must cry back into her self.

She has been gone for so long. She has been
the duck with webbed feet. She had held
his head. Everything, no fault of anyone,
she has suffered and cared. What can return
to her will return, maybe no thing she knew
but she asks for it, crying, the pond and
the dark house falling away.

Hunger

Setting out one day like every youth,
mostly because you are hungry,
you make the long journey away.
East of the sun, west of the moon,
you find the barrel that never ceases
its mead, the loaves replenished,
the gift of the dwarf
if you have the fool's luck. She
brings you a burnt orange chair
and the frame for a bed. She brings
two cans of carmine spray paint,
and each week, with her stubby thumb
and forefinger, she hands you the check
for your week's labor in her service.
Your feet are pink from paint
and in spite of the Mostly Good treatment,
you feel the loss of home.

But if you are not the fool,
the travel takes years longer
and the time without grain
or mead is almost unbearable.
You partake of the feast at last
only to learn you have stolen
without wit from the formidable ogress,
never, you say, knowing better,
and now she claims the right to eat

your first child and your last. She's
a regular Saturn, foaming and so on.

What about the horse who told you
his secrets or the toad that rose from the pond?
Was the nightjar not there on the moon?
You have always known better.
The tide came to your feet and your mother
begged you not to go. Weep and wait
a bit, Princess. Wrap your cold hands
in the rabbit and clasp them together for truce.

Or go. Consequence
is the immortal dragon, its fine wings,
veined with the shimmer of stars,
and though you go out each day
with your lame toothpick sword,
this is the duel you may never win,
though you be, as best you can, the hero, the hero, and the fool.

Moon Smoke

In the high southwest
beyond the cankering oak
above the third floor's roof
between chimney and branches
I watch an oblate moon
fidget behind wisps of smoke
from the witch's campfire.
Folks are tossing dust
into the coals; the smoke
rises like windswept clouds.
Somewhere a woman is dancing
in iron-hot shoes. She
is going to escape,
and the bright moon fades.

Oh Clown

Fret

Last night in the yard blank with snow,
I waited for my dog. Listening, I heard
what might have been a neighbor's hound,
but then knowing owl, I worried about its size. Why,
in the dark, could I hear crows scattering?
Fear kept a close watch on my wiry terrier,
and the wary ear listened for the silence
of the roosting neighbor chickens.
Also, I'd heard of a coyote in town.

Some nights I would give my first best wish,
the one pledged you by that first needle-pricked
star, for the cold to lift, for the dog to rush,
for hurry, finally for the town to dissolve
like a train reflected back to the bridge
in rippled water. I'd pick solitude
and the silver ram sparking the sky, no
part gone wrong, our dinner already warm

on the table, the persistent song of won'ts and musts
and the fear of what happens to some stranger
in the cold—the drunk's heart stopping, the two
children sledding then gone—not crowding
like any swarming through my brain.

Tent Worms

I.
Bats droop from occasional branches,
large and brown-gray as mulched leaves.
An old woman's hair hangs scalped above;
she twisted down the drain
and came out a clog. Each web holds
a dead winged female and one hundred eggs.

II.
In a story from *The Book*
of Stolen Images, the orphan boy
is nudged awake by the steady brown mare.

He rises in his white nightgown
and runs into the gloom startled
by the moon sliding behind white veils,
ice flaking down from the sky like lace.

What begins in pleasure, ends in fright.
No one ever misses him. The night
mare thunders and snorts, rears;
her eyes glow. He is trapped

in the bricked alley, the abattoir's
stink in the nearby trash. The brown
mare's nostril's flare. Her teeth,
her lips, the web of net—Oh God—

web shocks from her mouth and wraps
the terrified boy and he is gone.

Horse with the silk of spider in her throat,
her belly rises fat with boy for one moment only.

III.
Desperate sacks hang from bare trees.
Winter's ever wind won't pull
them down. The fluttering moth
of spring grows in this cold that drives
its future self toward light. Inside,

tucked into our cozy beds, dreamy
and disturbed, we begin to wish
for the crush of sparkling ice, the glistening
storm of crack in night, broken branches
and the murdered eggs, the woodman's ax,
or a story's end where each peaceful boy is born again.

"Or Someone He Had to Obey"

What generation hasn't forged belief from fear?
We close ourselves inside temperate buildings,

using the large world only when we have to,
for travel or for the hunt and play of woods.

We move in modified boxes, surrounded by steel.
We praise our ability to melt and cool metals.

We shape our world so the only religion
is the doctrine of dominion. Get the squirrel

out of the wall. Cage enough chickens
for every pan, tie the lamb's legs, and stew.

And then comes the night with its frozen thunder
and smashing trees. Ice suffocates the lines

and you fear what all is going dead. The trees
the neighbors planted long ago are proof of the loss.

You shiver inside layers of wool and plaster and brick
where your wee electronic devices glow a bit longer,

last remnants of the time before the crack and break,
before the shaking house, the rattled bones.

For months the trees remind us, stacked and stacked
at the curb, hanging broken in the air—

willfully, we move from cringe to irritation, waiting
too long for crews to haul away the broken proofs of fear.

This Face
This Face
This Face

— is a mouse's face looking
at me where I sit on the floor.

— is pale and a bit birth-
canal-smashed under blue cap,
lids closed.

— is drawn down in ways
that signal the forties.
Who ever knew, Helen Hunt,
we'd grow into those women?

— is drawn with pencils
and brushes, tattooed eye
liners, too flat eyelids.

— slack with fat, is corralled
in elastic bands
to press oxygen into the mouth
and nose.

O face, O hairy nostrils,
O clogged pore and scab,
O cracked or burning lips,
O tear leaking from the duct,
O cheeks never high enough,
clock, spring and wire,
mustache dressed with chili,

hint of ear under the hair
  you should brush back from your eyes,
bearded dog with wet black nose,
snort and unacknowledged sigh,
scar, burned flesh,
raised eyebrow, twisted lip—

think what we've created in your visage,
what names we've called
thanks to your expressions.
Let no one say the teeth and no one
call the sockets. We want skull
obscured by flesh. Even
the fearsome mouse looks and runs like hell.

Surveillance

I am being followed by raccoons.
The first one crossed slow
through neighborhood traffic,
stopping the southbound
and then the northbound car
which swerved and went around.
She stopped in front of our passenger tire
and looked at me. Drive on, I said,
drive. That thing was big
as a coatimundi, the neighborhood
ideologue later said. I was watchful
all night and wore tall boots when I walked.

If she'd been an old woman under a cloak
of stripe and ringed eyes, I'd have known her
sooner for the specter that she was,
warden, watcher, or that old white opossum
that once showed its teeth against the sliding glass.

I am walking on the shore when
raccoon comes, small, gray, cute even
until he looks right at me and comes a step closer.
Go away; go the other way.
Everyone realizes it's just me he wants,
so I put the three books of poetry I carry
spines down in the sand,
a barrier wall to confuse him. I flee,
losing the library copy of Glück's *Ararat*
to the wild. They keep doing this,
I shriek to whoever will listen,

third one this week:
                    Raccoons
are trying to get me. In the hunched back
of the largest one, she carried age
like a contagion. Soon, claw fingers will wave
come here, come here. You, with your baby
high cholesterol, with your blood
pressure just up enough. You're slow,
you're one of us. Put on the cloak, slow down,
grub through the corn cobs
and the leftover breads. Take this white
pill, this pink. Swallow, swallow
with your morning juice, come hump
along the shore and the street with us.

Little Skulls

"the vertebrae are absolutely undeveloped skulls"
—*from* Moby Dick

We say, *My back*,
Oh, my neck. We say,
Bone spur, *Pinched nerve*,
Nerve, but the spine
knows better. Each bone
pieced in its column
is a skull not quite finished
forming. The little heads
must have their language
of desire. If only I, one
might think. If only I,

says C2. *Arrarow, arrarough*,
they whisper from the bed,
pressed flat into the sheet
again. Each not-quite
mouth is death plucked
from the graveyard,
Hamlet's foil in his palm,
Tibetan yak bone beads
pressed into hands
for prayer. The body
simpers along, one more
dampened life form

in the long line of planets,
swirl of galaxy, world
within world, aborted
head, turned corner. We pay
with pain for selection,

that too simple word
for denial, that flip
side of unformed, re-used,
up- or down-cycled,
needed, but unfortunate
as any thing aspiring.

Once

after a painting by Hugo Simberg, 1903

Two boys slingshot the winged girl,
watched her fall, bound
her broken head, wiped blood
from her impossible wing,
and built a stretcher to carry her home.
Industrious brave sad-eyed brats.

They wondered who'd beat
them down to their knees,
be it father or elder, their God
or some other. She
clutched the stretcher with hands stained
from the fall and the gripping earth.

We can punish them now,
call them adults in spite of their size,
send them to prisons or hold them to death,
and meanwhile their parents
and elders, their God and their world
will go right on failing,
pulling more children like angels
from sky and the earth to graves in the dirt.

And Kidsley Divey, Too

Lilliebelle, 1920-1935

Mairsy dotes and dosey dotes and little
lambsy divey. Lilliebelle is underground. We
keep her under ivy. The hired hand
was like a man and fondled her forever.

The hired man had lots of hands and
Lillbelle's under ivy.
Her mother wrenched her by the arm. Her
mother slapped her daughter. The hired man
said that's ok and Lillbelle's under ivy.

Mairsy dotes and dosey dotes and little
lambsy divey. The doctor cut and some just bleed
without hospital help, just bleed.

We legislate her underground. We keep
her under ivy. Lilliebelle went to the ground
and left one name behind her.

Smashing the Clown

First we blew him up with a pump
until his red nose came unstuck from his face,
then I thought of you
sticking your tongue out, saying
almost singing, *compromised, compromised.*
I made my fist the way my mom taught me
when I was four—never put your thumb inside.
She knew stuff like that. I pulled back
in a way no one had to explain,
right hook, I think, or uppercut.

I'm five foot six inches and the clown's
just over four. He's going to get it
in the snout from me every time,
pathetic squeaker, smiler, red-headed
Bozo. I smack him down
and he comes back up simple enough
never to be annoyed. Oh
clown, oh vinyl bop containing multitudes,
I can't be more than three
while I stand here eager
for you to swing back up for the second fist.
I'm taking on your grin, going back
like you for another turn, son of a bitch.

I Refuse to Think about the Death Penalty

In what used to be the garden,
oak leaves are caught amongst
the spiked yellow fronds of iris.
So far the sage has sheltered
this year from frost. Sometimes I think
about teasing into the daylily foliage
with a red rake that would rip those blades
that still grow. All the neighborhood
is layered, leaf over grass. We
are a treed people. Imagining gardening,

daytime neighborhood, the nylon shells
of snowmen or Santas lie
like litter in browned up yards.
I read about the prison's waiting room
where a mural shows Elijah rising,
Daniel afraid while the lion's eyes
violate whoever looks away
from a man who surely never knew enough.
Surely, his family sits with him.
Surely, his mama prays
from the God book. Perhaps,
they have done this before,
then stayed, and unstayed, go again
years later.
    I thought
the Springtime resurrection
of the lilies and irises suited
better than religion's metaphor,
that the nighttime illuminated

idols would suffice for religion,
but I see now we're all caught up
in divinity and justification.

On Becoming a Snake

i.
I remember the tank and the heat lamp,
the stripped branch and the stones.

ii.
I am riding a black cat through the night.

iii.
My skin is almost bloody with scales
and turning toward scale. Whatever
of the earth I give, I am the whole
shiver of exoskeleton and scalp.

iv.
The dream of arms has left us.
Everything quakes and we writhe.
Upwards upwards, all movement
proceeds from the eye.

v.
I miss my rounded tongue most.
Never the ache of thigh, never
the dry winter pressing, but the clack
in the back of the cheek,
the glottal and the stop—oh,
the sorrow of only this this this

vi.
You might kill me with a brick.

Trapped Miner

I wanted it to birth me out to the earth again
so I told the mine I had great power. Each day,
I harnessed myself like an ox, and pulled.

The moon was a memory but the dirt
glowed like mica.

Above and Below

Under the drifted snow, dirt,
and the diligent roots of grasses.
Above, the squirrel bridging
the gap with its digging. Birds
make shadows in air.
Everything is white and not white.

Under the earth, a cave,
limestone pillars, and the stored goods
of winter folk. Above the earth,
this house, and the stocks
we've set ourselves of flour and egg.
Trucks roll up from inside the earth,
and few notice more than entrance ramp.
No one happens to think, *Exit
ramps for the underworld!*

Lower than the temperate cave, tunnels,
crevices, rooms we no longer
have patience to mine. Up above,
revolving restaurants, towers designed
for the brag. Higher, the drone.
Lower again, the sediment, mantles, cores.
The planet cloaks itself in regolith.

Satellite and stars, galaxy,
liquid iron, heat you always suspected.
As above, so below,
but all the facts dissolve
no matter what we think we know.

Some of us must go down
and teach the earth of our power.
You might harness yourself like an ox
to pull rocks through that skyless world
or let your flute song wake
the bones. Then the sphere will birth
you out again, like the crocus
that doesn't fear even the snow.

Ritual & Meditation

I open the back door and send out the dog.
No idea is a bad idea, I think tonight,
looking outside into midnight, one light illuminating
the garden patch where the elves' hats
of echinacea seeds cone their dark stems.
I have left them waist-high, sharp
and dark as insidious tribal darts.
My good dog arches his long back
to moisten the freezing ground. My husband
is long asleep, his bedtime crossword
already haunting his dreams. Words
fill in the spaces of his shallow sleep.
I have spent the last days of the week
charred or smoldering. The sharp air
of January seeps down from the door's head.
The neighborhood rooster is long quiet.
I hear the cat's bell, and the dog comes on.
We move into the warm spaces of the house.
I think fondly of magic, ready to keep this calm.

The First Dog

Antidote for Winter

I.
I want our house sitter
to defend the closet with a spear.
I want her to clamber up in the night
when she sees the beams
of flashlights passing the floors.

I want her to hold
the thief by the throat
for this is the epitome of performance,
true lust for the job.

II.
I want my student
to forgo the 6-hour energy,
to sleep soundly each night for nine hours.
I want him to amuse me
with talk of Nantucket.

He should believe *come a stove boat*
and stove body when they will,
for stave the soul, Jove himself cannot.
I want his mind unleashed
and sane in its own time.

III.
I want my short-legged dog
to bark and bounce when the black
cat leaps mewing with sleep to the bed.
I want the dog one step too far

down down off the edge,
too eager, too fast,
while the cat curls around
on the bed too tall for the poor dog's return.

I want the dog all teeth and white eyes
and game for the chase from sleep
into wake for this is the terrier's perfection,
wagging back to us even at 3 a.m.

           ✷

I want what I want: the spear and the noise
and the bright light shining from the mind to the soul.
I want the gash healed and the little furnace blasting.

Gift

The arm appears from under the water's surface.
The arm holds the green and silver sword.

The sword appears from under the water's still silver.
The hand grasps the bronze hilt, prominent knuckles.

Truth arrives from that blank green lake
like Venus served by rippling ocean,

rising gently, as though breaking from one world
into the next were no more difficult than breath.

Mimicking the action backwards, you break
the crème brûlée, tapping your small silver spoon
against burned sugar held in a crystal cup.
This stanza is the mistake, the move
to the spoon, to the surface broken from above.

I was not talking about the drilled earth,
the surgeon's scalpel, the axe wedged into the wood.

I was leading you to the small leg's kick,
to the reaching arms, to the hand's unwavering grasp.

Mr. Redbud

Mr. Redbud, I'm not sure how
well you can hear me anymore.
You're the moon through a telescope.
I'd like to hang a plastic Easter
egg on each one of your limbs.
Oh Mr. Redbud, wait, wait,
and now you bud. To hell
with the rain, and to hell with your roots;
everything's going to be okay.

Helloooo, Helloooo, Mr. Gravity,
are you there? I wanted to tell you
about the buzzards out at the farm.
They almost live on the pole out
by the old cellar. You could dive
in there during a storm, grab hard
to the ground and hang on.

Dear Mr. Red Dirt, you have ruined
the white canvas shirt, the one
with the chainsaw grease on the sleeve.
I fear putting it in the washer
with anything but jeans. Also,
you've eaten away the rubber soles
of my best go-to-hike boots,
though, I admit, burrs
stuck pretty bad in their thick laces.
I request restitution forthwith.

Oh, Grasshopper, how you hop
so fast into morning. Coffee
and laundry, the clean dishes,
maybe a poem. Oh Grasshopper,
when will you ever learn?
You took those ants too much to heart.
The freezers are full. Winter
is nearly over. Sing or snore,
come ʿa rain come ʿa rain come ʿa kinebo
kinebo sinebo karo saro
rattletrap pennywinkle popadoodle yellowbug
come ʿa rain come ʿa rain come ʿa kinebo,
and stretch your lean limbs slow,
hug the big trunk of a foreign tree,
have piccolo gelato, afternoon espresso
when you need to wake up.
The raked leaves will wait for tomorrow
or for the good and neighborly wind.

At last, Mr. Bigmouth
Bass, remember the time
we bobbed on our toes,
took stride against the current,
and rode the breakers into shore?
We've been king of the sea,
king of the pond and the shore.
Oh Mr. Bigmouth, let's play
with the line and the pole,
let's eat plates decorous
as ballrooms, one course

after the next, bubbles
for me, martini straight up
with olives, of course, for you.

Come on, Mr. Coldbones,
let's all go to bed.
I've got the black kitty
that sleeps on your feet.
Come on, Mr. Coldbones,
let's all go to sleep.
I've got the black kitty,
and that's all that she said.
If you want to hear more,
you can sing it yourself.

Riding the Takayama Train:
What I Can and Cannot Name

Rice paddies, bamboo, rich texture of pine,
the tall bamboo stalks, trees I cannot name,
all the usual behind-the-town leftovers, rail car
and track, the unwindowed backs of businesses,
lavender slacks among many balconies hung with laundry,

no graffiti (the rich characters decorating signs
and walls are its official substitutes).
On toward Tokyo, our first pagoda
floats against the near horizon.

Strong spring sun hits the windows high and hard.
Squinting against gray pulled shades,
I see a graveyard of television antennas
on roofs leveling against our tracks.
                                    River.
Rail bridges, industrial this and that, tractor,
occasional man walking fields, a color
I soon call Tokyo blue, both dark and bright,
on this falling-in barn,
on that apartment, that business.

A city never much shows itself to the rail.
Here a lone house before the wood, five
blooming plums line the ledge.

This train is only the quick line of knowing,
not half an alphabet, less than a schoolgirl's primer.
Then my eyes turn toward the duck,
a bird I recognize, floating, like any duck
before our small and agreeable world.

In the Heart of Life

I. Going Up Mountain

Going up mountain,
    daffodils become snow.

Diesel train to Takayama:
    plum blossom, Kiso River,
    tunnel.

The Kiso and train
    trade spaces,
switch back switch back
    bridge and track.

At a place where
the Kiso pools,
    not yet to the fields
    of tea bushing into ready leaves,

all mountain and tree
    grown straight line,
clear-cut and replanted,
everything inverts into
    the river:
watch the train under
    our train under
    water, a yellow glow, move.
Scarecrow scare. Seedling grow.
    Watch the rapeseed grow.

II. Down Mountain

Cherry blossom meets plum,
green tea, topiary,
   daffodil garden,
uncut stones mark cemetery.

How soon we learn the sign
for exit, 出口. The rapeseed glows.
Even here, the footprints
of Persephone who was followed
by the snouts then tails of trailing
herded pigs.

Tale

We're taught the value of careful
wishes from childhood stories, so
we can't help believing

though we fight the notion

that our thoughts must come
to something, that we hold powers
beyond our control. The fisherman's
story that lands his wife dead

and him in the original poverty,
or the king's idea of wealth that kills
his daughter, or the bride's need
of her seven brothers all linger

in the blue of story's edge.
The uncle lies gasping and choking
in the hospice bed with breathing

violent enough to pitch him
to a floor he couldn't get up from.
His wife is losing. His children
have taken the shifts they can.

Be careful: it's coming in
its own time, and your terrible wishes
and your trained prayers
can't hardly change the anatomy
of their place or of yours.

Dreaming the Graveyard Ivy

I had to ask you to pull off the blue and green leech
because I couldn't rip it off my thigh. I told you
the hilarious story of the ivy that grew up
under my trench coat and out the collar.
I wasn't even itchy. When I woke up, I thought

about the minister calling her the wrong name,
her unmarried name, and how for sixty-some-
odd years or so she'd thought of herself as married—
if Billy were alive today
                                    he'd be the only one
here that knew her in that name. She was in her coffin.

We used to go to his grave when it was new
and plant ivy to cover the mound. It would take years
to make the earth and plant remember him.
Back then people could stand sadness. We stood
each time in rain by green canopies. Cars made
an inappropriate backdrop. Someone
always dared to honk at our grief.

Manners sometimes drive the day. Even
in the dream, I didn't scream about the blood
creature on my thigh. I know what the ivy's for
and which grave I never covered. Maybe
they won't let us plant anymore. The alternative's neglect:
the same as staggered breaths that stopped
for just a second every time
the only person who never knew her
stood and called her by the name, obscene
as muttering in seats but never making a scene.

Memory, Our Enemy

Imagine you can bring your grandmother
back from the dead. There she stands
at the stove, a can
of Blue Ribbon hidden in the range.

Her mother sips Mogen David
in the upholstered chair.

Now you've done it,
resurrected Great-Granny, too:

expect a flood of green glasses
for the blind, dreamsicles, alligator
bags filled with pennies, the one
that broke while you held it out
and spun, spun circles in the grass,
copper circles flying, lost and laughing:
a first lesson in centrifugal force.

    Feeble memory can never be enough.
    Thinking like this, I'm mad enough
    to hold the book and sing the hymn,
    to understand your Eden and the punishing God.

If you don't know memory's failings now,
just wait until the first dog dies.

Friend Monkey

My aunt lost her favorite scarf on the plane
because I puked. The plane circled waiting.

For years I studied the low fence, the monkey's
long arm stretched to the branch, the bluing ink.

The monkey was my friend. He made eyes.
I was so young I don't know what I remember.

He was thin as the bare branches he climbed.
And the keeper poked him or prodded with a stick

working an electric charge to teach him down
and not out; Washington Zoo, 1968. I cried.

Looking at our album, I learned this story:
my fault for ruining the scarf, or no,

the plane, how unusual it was then not to land.
Our first flight, just 153 miles from home,

the earth squared off yellow and green below.
For years I felt the cruelty toward that animal.

The plane's circling had something to do
with riots. That's all I ever heard

until today when looking for the year, I found
the four days after King's assassination.

History was a scarf and puking and tears.

Rooted

"In the kingdom of bang and blab." —*Theodore Roethke*

In the battle between trees and men,
the tree grows itself down into the earth
claiming an immobile hold.

When the plane goes down
over an "*Ir-*" country, the uniformed brother
dies again.

Elder brothers find a long board
in their old barn. They will go out
to the creek's edge, rope around
one waist, and lever against
the cut tree that wouldn't fall.

In 32 hours of rain, can the severed wood
reattach itself, roots and trunk in earth,
limbs stretched skyward?

They leave the creek bed full of dead.
Bad cypress, thin-rooted, dry and threat.

The nucleus of the old man is still pushing
against the tree. And the tree won't move;
it can't. Soldier, soldier, mourning the
soldier. Trees and grief. The strong push
against immutable bark. Fifty years
young brother gone. Sap and scrape
on his hands.

Honey

After the dog ate the hive,
he hurt and shat bees for a week,

but the sweet comb drew him
with its waxy buzz and dripping love.

And then the tenaciousness of a terrier,
which he was not, not even part,

but still, knowing someone fought him
for this food, drove him to speed.

Like that, chomp, and it was gone, the sweet
sting and sting and sting. Oh, honey,

oh poisonous bees, or pop bottle
shaken with cold pills, ball of fire,

everlasting sex, the hunger and the anger,
all the kids locked out of the room.

Spring

Spring lashes upon us. Who has
not fallen in love with a single flower?

Who has not lusted after the yellow crocus's
saffron bursting against snow?

And when the high winds come dropping dead
limbs into our driveways,

weren't we cheering on the storm?

Smashed arm on the rail track,
almost identifiable as human.

The gush of oil thickening fish.
Broken Earth, broken flower.

Rain trapping us in our skin and mold.
    Don't sneeze, the shooter might hear you.

The Eldest Son

journeyed to seek his fortune. His parents
had wished him well, had even offered him home,
but he must go and so he did until

                        a kingdom,
weeping king, lost princess, where
he served with no particular distinction
for a year. And then the ubiquitous
and fateful visit home
where he found at once his parents grieving,
his brothers working the mares on the hill,
his sister safe in her bed, the fields full,
and his inheritance fully lost
for he had come home
to find himself dead.

The year and the work
had taken him somehow or other. To be sure,
they all recognized and welcomed him with feast,
split the pink pig on a spit, pulled crackling
over hot coals, and heard his story about haystacks
high as the glass hill wherein she hid,
but he was the dead son for whom his parents wept.

The princess is neither here nor there in this tale.
She may become a loaf or a banded duck.
She may quake at the knife or the gun
or live breathless for her hours at embroidery,
but she is neither here nor there in this tale
of the son who leaves and returns and finds himself dead,
in this tale of the hero who creeps out of heroics.

What shall he do with his death?
Shall he make himself a terrible bear
with claws like swords and sabered teeth?
Will he go into the wood and smite trees?
Should the meadow mares hide their foals?
He will wear the cloak of a thousand days.
He will hide in the book of all words. When
the time comes to greet him, will he go
like a clod to the dirt? Have no fear and have fear
for he comes with two clips and despair.

Another Story

begins where the earth begins
long ago west of the moon
    She is woebegone without mother
    and he is woebegone
    as any father doomed to marry.
    What magic makes the man
    reveal his daughter's grit?

    She walks the soles through
    three pair of iron shoes,
    keeps every chicken's bones
    in her sack. The stepmother
    beats her, towers her,
    mocks her in the ash. Father
    marries her to the boar,
    the stoat, ogre, genii,
    murderer, handsome-one-
    whose-mother-will-eat-
    her-children, keeper of the keys.

When the story ends
and the century passes,
    she has lost her shoes,
    her hair, walked the earth away
    from her father, been buried
    to her neck, chopped up
    and resurrected. She
    holds her child to her breast,

takes from her sack
the chicken bones and climbs
the ladder they make until
one wrung short she
chops off her little finger
to reach the door
                          that ends
the story, breaks the evil,
makes wrong right, and so

they live happily until they die,
while the wicked end badly,
tied to a raging horse,
which if it has not stopped
is running still.

Forgotten One,

you are the funnel cloud that drops
over the highway, then slips back into the sky.

You are the cat's one stitch
left in her belly. You

are the stepsister chained to the wall
with her bowl full of tears.

You yap along in your sleep
and your leg dog-twitches.

When you look out the window, you hear
the big moon howl like a train crossing road.

When the sinkhole opens, you
are the one taken like a building into the gap
everyone gawks at,

finally no longer forgotten
by the only universe that ever mattered.

Snouts and Bristles

Body

Something is in my body
like the North Pacific trash heap
too far away to clean up or to bother.

I am trying to stay asleep
because it is not yet my morning.
Something is in my body

organ-deep, crawling up toward skin.
Not cancer (though I fear) just pain.
First under my rib, the ocean

crawls with its dangerous plastic.
I turn and the tortoise turns
into my kidney, into my lung.

Body, don't pleurisy me. Body,
don't pain. Let the albatross
die on mistaken lunches,

let the vortex keep
what can't spit up. Pain
recycle your own pain.

✳

Pain insists, but the planet
is more subtle.

＊

Live on this ocean's indelible lump
when you die. When
the continents long fail, this.

＊

One of these won't be ignored.

Tropes Long Since Gone

Millpond, spinning wheel, frog, sword, scythe,
wheat crop, hut, very old man,
good little mother, pot, stew
the idea of service, the long journey from home.

I will do your bidding for the years
you have contracted. I will dig
into the dirt with a garden spade,
pile hay in a stall, bury the gold
ring under the farthest stone in the field.

Only a bird can break this service,
the one who drops the wing's feather
I might catch before it touches ground.

For this, babies pay with their lives.
For this, children are left in the wood.
For this, girls may be raised in the eagle's nest,
boys in the company of fairies or trolls.
For this, your strongest wish (the child
that never grew) might be granted.

For this, women are chained to the wall,
men to the backs of horses. Gold
and silver and the backs of thieves.
Rain that comes for a century. Toil
spindles along.
                    When we gave up service,

we gave up the good earth, we left

spent rods suspended in the living earth.
In this tale, the witch and the troll, the ogre
and the fool come late. My life
had been a plaything where even the food
was sweet and fat as reward.
                           We left
the idea of service with the old wife
standing at the door and the fish
hiding under the rock. The gold ring
was never buried. The wishes,
granted without being wished,
were too obvious. Any life lived
in idleness inevitably calls forth
the beaks of a thousand birds,
their two thousand talons, all leaning
in and melting upon the flesh,
the dream collapsing like a gilded age,

the old earth raising her thumb.

Speaking Likeness

I've never heard a cough quite like his
though my neighbor barked loud through cinder
block walls. In all this talk of dust

why is it we never remember the ash,
burned and not quite gone? Smear
your face with grief. Let the portraits
sing from the walls. The Renaissance blonde

is upon us, but she will not deign to greet
the one who opens the door. Some things
are past telling: the tramp on broad wings
who flies into the sunset, the names

of butterflies engraved on the planet's crust:
red admiral, blue admiral, funereal
duskywing, spotted Bermuda, pink
Amazon, Chinese yellow. Even the cabbage
alights on a leaf. I said *sunset*, I said *cough*,
grief, *past*, *dust*. Bark then, and we're done.

Your Albums

i.
I'm reading my news feed when I see
her chest tube wound, the raw space
she'd talked about as serious injury. When
her ribs broke, they punctured the lung.

This small circle of violence breathed.

ii.
Someone tells me we live in a visual culture,
that it's hard for students to travel.
They've seen it before they arrive,
so only the difficulties impress. But this one,
when I looked at her Ireland
green and stone, the ruins of fortress,
cathedral, castle, the last difficulties of an age,
I saw for the first time, her smile.

iii.
The babyfat happy child in the kiddy pool
has a prognosis of two years unless . . .
I've never met her parents. The parents I know
feed new foods to six-month-olds
and float them in duck rafts, recording
even the bows rubbing their hair, even their frowns.

iv.
Amidst the freehand ducks and the close-up
shots of cornbread, the still lifes
with Ethiopian inerja and tibs, the cracked

claw of a red crab with roasting ear, a dog
cuddled almost under the husband crashed out on the couch,
the farmer's market or backyard haul
of August tomatoes and Anaheim peppers, I
think I've come to see what you mean.

Trestle and Embankment

I.
The lone whistle proves the buzzing June
just like the sudden light of dusk's first fireflies.
Every transplanted strawberry wilts in the yard.

II.
I sleep so strong in the heat, it takes a ladder to climb out
again, or no, the soft footholds and handholds in the rift or cliff,
where someone has struggled out before me. Night
changes everything, even our room
where the sheets are made over in marzipan stars.

Our old dog coughs again like a grandmother
who has eaten too much eggplant too late in the evening
so my dreams take me into noise and daylight, a scene
of bees decorating the air with their sound and their swerve
as close to us as the redbud's gnarled limbs.

III.
Other times awake, I watch you breathe, your eyelids roll.
The train has stopped again in the middle of town.
Someone pressed himself across the tracks and stopped.
Everything is still now
after the train's lonesome push and the screaming brakes.

IV.
Each late night alone before sleep, reading while you sleep,
or fretting over the life's work unmade, the six chores
undone, I think I would prefer the promise of morning
where my best friend runs six or seven miles

before her children cuddle to her and the eggs cook
sticking in the pan. She's seven hours in,
when I wake. You're settled in work
when I join the day. Morning breaks me into pieces
and every organ speaks its subtle resistance. No
wonder I never embrace the time of the birds and the dew.

Tomorrow the newspaper will explain the waylaid train,
the broken man's last idea. I will imagine
the conductor's terror and hopelessness in the night
while you slept in hot air, and I kept watch,
knowing the stars, knowing the lives
that move in darkness, the sphere
that breathes when the sun moves away.

Losing Your Place

I forget that some currents bring cold,
and when I finally get in past my belly
I tell you "bracing"—*bracing*, as if
I've just discovered the word. Lifeguards
sit with their feet up on white or yellow stands,
umbrella-ed in these days of SPF and UVB.
We are in it up to our necks; the salt
lets us squat so our joints don't realize.
I think of my friend who couldn't walk up stairs.

I like sand that feels like a floor. Light brown
or tan, compact as eczema's circle when you feel it.
I wonder sometimes if the lake people who fear sharks
know the absence here of squish between the toes,
if this could make a difference. I think
they imagine the ocean as limitless darkness
something like a grave or the last pinpoint of light
blinking closed, jilting, and sharks as ubiquitous
and fierce as alligator snappers.
I stand on ground I can't feel shift.

Almost always the current lets us lean against it,
so we walk instead of stand to keep our place
straight out between the two markers: lifeguard,
and bag, bright umbrella, or stack of rafts. Today
it's the yellow flag of caution to the left.
This tide rips against my shins while I march
march march with my whole body, keeping place
by movement.

I dive under to look. I like
to remember that saltwater doesn't burn, that open eyes
have their place here. I anticipate shafts
of green light, perhaps mica flecks, minnows
schooling past, light refracting, but I'm startled
in the diving instant when the plank of me
goes backwards not forwards. I surface quickly,
braced again against what lets me.

Breaking Down the Body /
The Body Breaking Down

"as they do hills about Boston to fill up
some morass in the Milky Way."—lines from a novel

I.

Child, they've tied one arm to your body.
They've put the clown patch over your left eye.

II.

And you, you're listing to the lee side and also to the west.

Take the fist, fingers balled, or what was the fist.
The slipshod pinky slowly spilling out, leaking silver change
over the counter so it drops back to the silver chute.

Take the face, take the care you take, barely a smile
behind your plasticized mask. Take plasticity

and throw it into the sea. We'll break down the body
into the ligament reconfigured like a bunion,
the callous and the neuropathic heels. Your shuffle,

drag, step, ball, shuffle, iron chain, and unsignified
glance is compensation for the dance. The earth
might be *an empty cipher, except to sell by the cartload*

and the simplest limb restricted might as well be a star
shooting down through the roof . . .
                                   You can't treat
Parkinson's like a lazy eye or stroked out arm.
The bowels might stop up like a rusted on screw

until its head's worn out. The seawater floating above
is your own wet air filling up the lung.
What doesn't kill you makes you wish
for something else that will.

                III.
                    Let the babies
struggle against the straps and patches. Let
the playground bastards point and throw sticks.
Every obstacle is the whale and every obstacle is the bone
we follow with our hooks and spears. There's the glow
of oil in the lamp. There's the glow of radiant pink
in the cheek, but the ships go down, the rigs explode.
The fish comes back with only you in his eye—
    why weary and palsy the arm at the oar, and the iron,
    and the lance? Behold, Oh Starbuck! for we go down
like Satan, taking a little heaven into our hells.

Penances   *or to be more specific,*
A List of Actions or States of Being and Corresponding, Often Unexpected, Penances

If you are going to roast the whole pig
in the barrel you sawed and hinged, welded,
bolted, wired, gouged, you must give up
your eyebrows and beard to the quick singe
and blast.
            If you are going to be pretty, expect
the long arm around your waist or wear
the wooden helmet clamped to your head.

If you are going to eat the pig
cooked in its whole, then like the jellyfish
who lost his shell for empathy, you'll lose
your shield of blonde.
                    If you are going to write
this poem or any hundred words, the black cat
will sink his deep incisors into your big toe
just to the point where you feel it. Watch
your knuckles.
            If you would have the rotten tooth
pulled clean from your mouth, expect to wake
shorn. Shiver in your little bed, short-haired
and devoid.
            Teeth and pig and the short hairs
of desire . . . honor your helmet and your shield;
even these some day might burst. Trade
almost anything away, the hair or tooth, the quick
blast of nerves' gasp, for your moments
of vigorous dominion, the roasted pig,
this sweet soft apple in your mouth.

Swallowing: Snouts and Bristles and the Hearts of Men

I was thinking of two thousand pigs, the earth-
shaking weight and terror of their stampede,
how at full run and near the steep cliffs
just this side of the Sea of Galilee, they might go on
into the water at full charge, barely realizing.

And after all that weight, wouldn't they love
the sea's effortless lift of hoof and heft? Pigs
can swim, and so maybe the first plunge,
though driven by terror, carried comfort, carried peace:
no more heat, the thick mud sloughing away,
the salt buoying them up and filling the mouth
with its sweetness and memory of blood.

But too many rushed in, and the sea keeps waves
and undercurrents. Their charge left no room
for turning back. Even if sea pigs feed on the mud
of the ocean floor, these swine were destined to swallow
infinitely and finally, so their whole bodies filled
with the acute pain of failed metamorphosis.
Gills or their like, would come in eons, never
in the last gasping moment when with water
their weight came back to own them.

Late, overtired, my head in solid ache,
I find the night's consistent pills. I imagine her desire
to reach for so many of these she'd slip
into their false care, so many she'd dissipate
into the hopeful lie of mist and vapor

over the weight of the earth and the sea.
I am aware, always squarely, piggishly inside this self.
No god can shift evil into the herd again.
I cannot run like the swine into the sea
rather than live with the demon and the spirit in me.

Storm

That cracking above us and the snap of limbs,
our trembling dog and the night lighting:
you asleep while the electronics blip and light
as they move from power to power. I have the desire
to see it all and also the will to sleep. Night storms
on like a hectic dream. The night is a vehicle
careening and reckless. We are wrecked
from the day, adrift in the stolid house. Whatever breaks
will wait until morning. Even the dog stills. We sleep
in the summer silence of lost power and surrender.
Even the dog forgets the gods of thunder and of rain.

Tears

"The rose remembers the salty waters" —*P. L. Travers*

When the house lifts into the sky,
the birds follow it. I needn't dream
of flying. I have the long stretch of arms
and the push of the sea for ballast.

Fairy dust or gold, the chipped shells
of a thousand fish, sparkle amidst dark,
against the untamed green of the algaed sea.

We remember a time without weight
when gravity was only constant pull and tug,
hair floating one way, the neck and feet another
and this was beauty. We lived on the diagonal,

never as now in the oversimplified drudgery
of constant pressing down
while our bodies do what they can, tiptoeing
with fetlocked heels, fighting down, fighting down.

The Right Answer

*"There was no reply to her question
and she did not expect one." —P. L. Travers*

I.
Climbing tall ladders they'd propped against the sky,
she watched the women paste gilt paper stars onto the air.

She had learned that tiny women with voices pitched
above whistles could break their fingers into sugar sticks;

that no amount of pampering, oysters, fresh cream, tartan
plaid overjackets, would make a small dog into a boy;

that even the vainest woman, one who checks her hat's roses
against the glistering shop window, could refuse, with a
    sniff, to speak;

that a steadfast chant and permanence of words feathered
    your ruff,
brought dove and pigeon warmth, the cooing nesting of
    your skirts;

that even Proper lives between hedges and sky and dances
the sailor's hornpipe and the highland fling when it will and
    sees the king;

that even dear mothers punish, panda standing her fur on end,
dolphin with her snout outthrust, polar bear with fangs.

II.
Are the stars gold paper or is the gold paper stars?
Do fallen stars list on the horns of a cow?
The child in blue cloth ripped from sky, the second

of the Pleiades, walks invisible stairs back up to its home.

Your parents resist at least twenty-eight thousand visions
of the truth. They're like the cow who believed each dandelion
either sweet or sour and not one moderately nice. But like any
        good Jane
you read your books, and find the stars and paper
                                as good as gold or gingerbread.

Because I Get Sick in a Boat and Feel Terror at Zero G-Force,
I Give the Poets These Suggestions Against Velocity

"In the 'time of inspiration' the poet flew from one world to another, 'riding on dragons,' as the Chinese said." —Robert Bly

Not the boat but the water,
not the rocking but the waves.
Marry the salt that carries you up
and the low green world without air.

Undersea, even your hair goes kelp
and twists like flirting snakes.
Mica, silt, sand, gold flecks this atmosphere
and nothing spits back into your eye.

No bracing against speed, no whipping,
no hands knuckled around a bar or rope cleat,
not the tracked seat of a rolling car,
not the propeller or throttle but the body
loose in its most essential of elements.

Riding a dragon, drift the hot white air,
let the smoke treat you like a comb jelly
hefted, untentacled, urged, and forged by the sea.

How We Travel

Because we live in the space in between,
we can't have a north hand or an east.
We travel by landmarks, the fifth red sign
after The Reef, the stoplight at Anchor Inn.
Even the stars might lead us on—keep
the moon holding water and Venus in repose
just over your left shoulder.

Looking up like this,
sometimes I see violence in the moon,
its cragged landscape the villain's face
where probably we left our metal and plastic waste.
The whale constellations followed long enough
lead to visions of motorcut manatees.
I have heard the motors' sinister whirr under
frilling waves myself, known surrender and surround.

Stars mirror shiplight on sea,
and the thrust of bilge that always seeps
like a galaxy behind our boats.
When I swam and came out green, algae
or worse leached to my skin in the everyday
canals and docks of the neighborhood.
That was only the beginning of understanding
how our end—the slimed creature
crawling on the stinking shore—
may come so terribly to resemble entrance,
the grasp and weight of our beginning.

Gratitude and Notes

Thank you to Caryn Mirriam-Goldberg for her encouragement and to Tracy Million Simmons and Linzi Garcia of Meadowlark Press for all their hard work. Thank you to my first readers, my friends and my poets, especially Allison Blevins, Melissa Fite Johnson, Katelyn Roth, Morgan McCune, Lori Martin, Josh Davis, Chris Anderson, and Roland Sodowsky. Thank you to my students and friends, too many to list, who have read my work, inspired me, and kept me writing.

Thank you to Mom, Barbara Lucas, and Dad, Donald J. Washburn.

The Book of Stolen Images includes many allusions and references and the occasional quote. In addition to newsworthy events, some of the poems' images and words recall or pay homage to:

> Andrew Lang's *The Orange Fairy Book, The Yellow Fairy Book, The Crimson Fairy Book, The Red Fairy Book, The Violet Fairy Book*
> Grimms' Fairy Tales
> The works of P.L. Travers including all the *Mary Poppins* books and *Friend Monkey*
> Herman Melville's *Moby Dick*
> Marianne Moore, "toadstools slide, each on the other"
> Robert Bly's essays and poems
> *Bedknobs and Broomsticks*
> Carol Frost
> Anne Sexton
> Robert Frost

The Brothers Grimm
A folk chorus remembered by my husband from
    "Froggy Went a'Courtin'"
The folk rhyme and later song "Mairzy Dotes"
James Baldwin's "Sonny's Blues"
Katherine Anne Porter's "The Jilting of Granny
    Weatherall"
William Stafford's "Traveling through the Dark"
Flannery O'Connor's "A Good Man Is Hard to
    Find"
William Faulkner's "Barn Burning"
Katherine Mansfield's "Miss Brill"
Sister Helen Prejean & research on the death
    penalty from a variety of news sources

Both "Trapped Miner" and "Above and Below" share an image I remember hearing from a rescued Chilean miner on NPR. I consider "Trapped Miner" a found poem.

I dedicate the poem "Peace and Reckoning" to Robert Hass, with part "iii" dedicated to Norman Dubie.

"I Refuse to Think about the Death Penalty" is dedicated to Kristy Magee.

"Rooted" is dedicated to the Sodowsky brothers.

"Mr. Redbud" is dedicated to my husband, Roland Sodowsky.

✳

    As the United States enters a dark and dangerous time for women and for health care professionals, I offer a longer note on the poem "And Kidsley Divey,

Too" which takes its inspiration from newspaper accounts of the tragic death of Lilla Belle or Lilliebelle Davies who died in 1935 at age fourteen.

In 1935, Dr. Anna Longshore, at sixty, was charged for at least the third time in her life with murder for performing an abortion on a woman or child who did not survive the procedure. Dr. Longshore did not go to prison on any of the charges.

The poem posits Lilliebelle's mother as angry and in charge. This may not be true at all. Her mother did eventually take her to the hospital where she died. But she never testified. She later changed her story completely, and the case against Dr. Longshore was dismissed.

The man who impregnated the child, Lilliebelle, was twenty-five. He said he'd been caressing Lilliebelle for a year before he had sex with her.

He said that in his suicide note. When he learned that Lilliebelle had died, he killed himself by gunshot. His note professed his love, put a time frame on what I would call his grooming, and said he had planned to run away with her but had "listened to poor advice." The families buried them in side-by-side graves.

Did the abused child have a say in whether she wanted an abortion or not? Her abuser, a worker on her parents' farm, seemed to have had some choice in the matter as he gave up one plan for another. I can imagine Lillibelle and her parents fearing for her were she to be taken away from her family pregnant at fourteen by the man who had sexually abused her.

Her mother took her to a hospital four days after the abortion. The following day she died of internal hemorrhage and septic peritonitis. Lilliebelle might have survived the abortion procedure had it been performed in that hospital.

.

Acknowledgments

The author wishes to sincerely thank the editors who first published and sometimes republished the following:

"And Kidsley Divey, Too" in *Santa Fe Writer's Project*

"Another Story" as "A Story" and "The Right Answer" in
    Moon City Review

"Body" in *Prime Number*

"The Eldest Son" in *Radius*

"Fret" in *I-70 Review*

"Honey" at *SWWIM Everyday*

"How We Travel" in *Red Rock Review*

"Hunger" and "Rooted" in *Pennsylvania English*

"In the Heart of Life" in *The Invisible Bear*

"I Refuse to Think about the Death Penalty" as "Refusal" in
    the program for Pittsburg State's 2012 Production of *Dead
    Man Walking*

"Little Skulls" in *Moon City Review*

"On Becoming a Snake" in *Cavalier Literary Couture* and in
    Dead Snakes

"Peace and Reckoning" in *Radius*; *OccuPoetry: Issue 2*, UC
    Davis edition; and in the program for Pittsburg State's
    2012 production of *Dead Man Walking*

"Penances" and "Ritual and Meditation" in *Ninth Letter*

"Philosophy" in *velvet-tail*

"Smashing the Clown" in *Midwest Quarterly*

"Swallowing: Snouts and Bristles and the Hearts of Men" and
    "Trapped Miner" in *Red-Headed Stepchild*

"Tent Worms" as "Winter, Tent Worms" in *Goblin Fruit*

"Trestle and Embankment" in *Whale Road Review*

"Tropes Long Since Gone" in *Flint Hills Review*

About the Author

Laura Lee Washburn is the Director of Creative Writing at Pittsburg State University in Kansas, and the author of *This Good Warm Place: 10th Anniversary Expanded Edition* (March Street) and *Watching the Contortionists* (Palanquin Chapbook Prize). *Harbor Review*'s chapbook prize is named in her honor, and she's the president of Small Harbor Publishing's Board of Directors. Her degrees are from Old Dominion University, where she interned for the *Associated Writing Programs Newsletter*, and Arizona State University. Born in Virginia Beach, Virginia, she has also lived and worked in Arizona and in Missouri. From her home in Pittsburg, Kansas, she edits *The Coop: A Poetry Cooperative*.

Meadowlark POETRY

Books are a way to explore, connect, and discover. Poetry incites us to observe and think in new ways, bridging our understanding of the world with our artistic need to interact with, shape, and share it with others.

Publishing poetry is our way of saying—

We love these words,
we want to preserve them,
we want to play a role in sharing them
with the world.

Meadowlark Press
— since 2014 —

meadowlark-books.com

Follow Meadowlark Press
on Facebook & Instagram

(f) **facebook.com/ReadAMeadowlarkBook**

(O) **@meadowlarkbooks**

www.ingramcontent.com/pod-product-compliance
Lightning Source LLC
Chambersburg PA
CBHW030957090426
42737CB00007B/570